Quiches

and Savory Tarts

Recipe	Page	Calories/serving	easy	fast	takes a while	good for guests	sophisticated	vegetarian	make ahead	inexpensive
Asparagus and Ham Quiche	6	600	●			●	●	◐	●	
Tomato Mini-Quiches	6	220				●	●			
Mushroom Tart	8	460	●			●	●			
Roquefort Quiche	9	550	●			●	●	◐	●	◐
Smoked Salmon and Leek Quiche	10	470			◐	●	●			
Tomato Quiche with Herbed Cheese	11	570				●	◐			
Shrimp Quiche with Saffron	12	450	●			●	●	◐		
Smoked Trout Quiche	12	610	●			●				
Gorgonzola Quiche with Pears	14	510				●	●	◐		
Smoked Fish & Fennel Quiche	15	460				●	●		●	
Corned Beef & Cabbage Quiche	18	1000							●	◐
Smoked Sausage Quiche	18	1190	●						●	◐
Broccoli Quiche with Turkey Breast	20	690				●			●	
Chili Pie	21	780	●			●				
Pork Tenderloin Quiche	22	830	●						●	◐
Cheeseburger Quiche	22	900	●			●	●			
Meat Loaf & Cabbage Quiche	24	890			◐				●	◐
Chicken Liver Quiche	25	700	●		◐	●	●			
Paté & Apple Tart	26	880	●			●				◐
Zucchini Mini-Quiches	30	410					●	◐		◐
Mushroom Quiche with Snow Peas	31	710	●				●	◐		
Curried Cauliflower Quiche	32	690					●	◐		◐
Eggplant Tart with Mozzarella	33	830			◐	●		◐	●	

Recipe

Recipe	Page	Calories/serving	easy	fast	takes a while	good for guests	sophisticated	vegetarian	make ahead	inexpensive
Carrot & Broccoli Quiche	34	650	●					●		●
Spinach Quiche with Feta and Olives	36	720			●	●	●	●		
Red Lentil Quiche	36	920						●		●
Shallot Quiche with Raisins	38	970				●	●	●		
Chinese Cabbage Quiche	39	690						●	●	●
Tuna & Garbanzo Bean Quiche	42	820	●				●		●	
Sausage & Sauerkraut Tart	42	530	●						●	●
Feta & Olive Quiche	44	870	●	●				●	●	
Two-Cheese Quiche	45	920	●	●			●	●	●	
Green Bean Quiche	46	600		●		●	●			
Corn Quiche with Smoked Sausage	46	770	●	●		●				●
Brussels Sprout Quiche	48	885	●			●			●	
Two-Mushroom Quiche	48	720	●				●	●		
Artichoke Tart	50	820	●	●			●			
Herbed Quiche	51	760	●					●		
Vegetable Tart with Gorgonzola	54	670				●			●	
Quiche Lorraine	54	960			●			●		
Tarte Provençal	56	700			●	●	●			
Pissaladière	56	690			●			●		
Camembert Tart	58	760			●					●
German-Style Onion Tart	59	860				●		●		
Middle Eastern-Style Lamb Tart	60	940			●	●	●			
Swiss-Style Cheese and Grape Quiche	60	845				●		●		

Table

Appetizers and Snacks

These savory tarts with luscious fillings are perfect as appetizers. What's more, they're easy to prepare in advance and you can coordinate the filling perfectly to complement the main dish. Don't make the filling too rich, though, or your guests will be full before the main meal is served. A small salad is the ideal side or garnish, such as a mixed green salad, including arugula, endive, and radicchio leaves. Or try an elegant mâche salad. Arrange the side salad next to the warm quiche.

Cute little bites

Mini-quiches don't just look cute—they're a great snack when you're entertaining a crowd and need a little something to offer with an apéritif. You can use any quiche recipe—simply divide the dough and filling among several smaller pans or ramekins before baking.

Tip! If you're in a rush you can buy ready-baked mini tart crusts at the supermarket or bakery. All you have to do is pour in a filling and bake for about 10-20 minutes until the filling is set. If you're cooking for company, make several of these little quiches ahead of time, pre-bake and freeze them.

A slice of quiche and a crisp salad—the perfect starter.

Always pans out great!

You can use practically any regular baking pan or dish to bake a quiche or savory tart. Most of our recipes are planned for a 10-inch round pan. If you use a pan with a smaller diameter, simply cut back on the filling.

Pie pan

A pie pan is usually metal, ovenproof glass, porcelain, or ceramic, with a smooth or fluted edge. You can serve and slice the quiche right from the pan.

Tart Pan

If you plan to bake quiche often, it's really worth investing in this practical pan. Usually metal, this pan is available with or without a nonstick finish. The pan has a fluted edge, but the bottom is separable so you can remove it easily along with the baked quiche.

Springform pan

This pan with a removable bottom and releasable sides should really be a standard kitchen item. It's not well suited for extra-soft, moist fillings.

Mini quiche dishes/pans

You can find small aluminum or tin pans and ceramic or porcelain tart dishes (or ramekins) in various sizes. The ceramic and porcelain ones are a tad more expensive than the same size in metal, but they actually do a better job of baking quiche. (The porcelain and ceramic pans are also available in larger 9- and 10-inch sizes.)

Casserole/lasagna pan

If you don't have a proper quiche pan you can also use a flat ceramic or ovenproof glass casserole pan that you'd normally use for lasagna or gratin dishes.

Broiler/baking pan

These pans are ideal when cooking for a crowd. Simply double the regular quiche recipe ingredients. It's best to line the tray with parchment paper for ease.

Asparagus and Ham Quiche

● sophisticated
● good for guests

Serves 6

Cream Cheese Pastry:
1 2/3 cups flour
4 oz cold cream cheese
4 oz cold butter
Pinch of salt

Filling:
18 oz asparagus
7 oz ham, fat trimmed
2 oz fresh chervil
1 3/4 cups crème fraîche
2 eggs
Salt & pepper to taste
1 tsp lemon juice

Prep time: 70 minutes
Per serving: 600 calories
18 g protein / 42 g fat / 40 g
carbohydrates

1 Put the flour in a bowl. Cut the cream cheese and butter into small pieces and add them to the bowl with the salt. With a fork, work the ingredients until the mixture resembles coarse meal. Dump the mixture onto a work surface and knead slightly until the mixture holds together (take care not to overwork the dough). Shape the dough into a disk and wrap with plastic wrap. Refrigerate the dough for 30 minutes.

2 Let the dough soften for 5-10 minutes. Lightly dust a work surface with flour. With a rolling pin, roll out the dough, starting from the center and moving to the edges, to an 11-inch circle, adding a sprinkling of flour when necessary to prevent sticking. Carefully transfer the dough to a 10-inch pan, centering it. With your fingers, smooth any wrinkles. Trim the dough edges even with the pan. Refrigerate until ready to use.

3 Preheat the oven to 400°F. Wash the asparagus and peel the lower third of each spear. Bring a large pot of salted water to a boil. Add the asparagus and cook for 10 minutes. Drain, plunge the asparagus into ice water, and drain well.

4 Chop the ham coarsely. Wash the chervil and strip the leaves from the stalks. In a blender or food processor, puree the ham, chervil, and crème fraîche. Blend in the eggs. Season with salt, pepper, and the lemon juice.

5 Lay the asparagus inside the crust. Distribute the ham mixture evenly on top of the asparagus. Bake until the filling is set and the crust is golden brown, about 30 minutes.

Tomato Mini-Quiches

● good for guests
● easy

Serves 6

Rich Pastry 1:
1 1/3 cups flour
3 1/2 oz cold butter
1 egg
Pinch of salt

Filling:
9 oz cherry tomatoes
3 green onions
3 oz Gruyère cheese,
  freshly grated
2/3 cup crème fraîche
2 eggs
Salt & pepper to taste
Freshly grated nutmeg to
  taste

Prep time: 55 minutes
Per mini-quiche: 440 calories
12 g protein / 30 g fat / 30 g
carbohydrates

1 Put the flour in a bowl. Cut the butter into small pieces and add it to the bowl with the egg and salt. With a fork, work the ingredients until the mixture resembles coarse meal. Dump the mixture onto a work surface and knead slightly until the mixture holds together (take care not to overwork the dough). Shape the dough into a disk and wrap with plastic. Refrigerate for 30 minutes.

2 Let the dough soften for 5-10 minutes. Lightly dust a work surface with flour. With a rolling pin, roll out the dough, starting from the center and moving to the edges, until it is about 1/8-inch thick, adding a sprinkling of flour when necessary to prevent sticking. With a large round dough cutter, or inverted jar or drinking glass, cut out six 5-inch circles, Carefully transfer the circles to 4-inch pans. With your fingers, smooth any wrinkles in the dough. Trim the dough edges even with the pans. Refrigerate until ready to use.

3 Preheat the oven to 400°F. Remove the stems from the tomatoes. Briefly plunge the tomatoes into boiling water to loosen the skins. Remove the tomato skins and halve the tomatoes. Trim and wash the green onions, and chop finely.

above: Tomato Mini-Quiches
below: Asparagus and Ham Quiche

4 In a bowl, stir together the cheese, crème fraîche, and eggs. Season with salt, pepper, and nutmeg.

5 Distribute the cherry tomatoes and the green onions among the crusts. Pour the cheese mixture evenly on top and bake until the filling is set and the crust is golden brown, about 20 minutes.

Tip! For ease, put the filled mini-quiches on a baking pan before putting in the oven.

Mushroom Tart

● good for guests
● easy

Serves 6
Rich Pastry 1, page 6
16 oz thick-sliced smoked
  bacon
1 tbs canola oil
1 large onion
26 oz mushrooms
1/4 cup dry sherry (or
  chicken stock)
Salt & pepper to taste
1 bunch fresh chives
4 oz Comté or Gouda
  cheese, freshly grated

Prep time: 70 minutes
Per serving: 460 calories
14 g protein / 26 g fat / 40 g
carbohydrates

1 Make the pastry and use it to line a 10-inch pan. Refrigerate until ready to use.

2 Dice the bacon. Heat the oil in a large skillet over low heat. Add the bacon and fry for 5 minutes. Peel and finely dice the onion and sauté with the bacon until the onion is translucent, about 5 minutes.

3 Trim and thinly slice the mushrooms and sauté with the bacon and onion for 10 minutes. Add the sherry and season with salt and pepper. Sauté until most of the liquid has evaporated. Remove from the heat.

4 Wash and finely chop the chives. In a bowl, mix the chives with the mushroom mixture, adding half of the cheese.

5 Preheat the oven to 400°F. Distribute the mushroom filling evenly in the crust and sprinkle the remaining cheese on top. Bake for 35 minutes, until golden brown.

Serving suggestion: Try this with Spicy Red Pepper Sauce, page 29.

Roquefort Quiche

● sophisticated
● make ahead

Serves 6
Basic Pastry:
1 1/3 cups flour
3 1/2 oz cold butter
5 tbs water (or white
  wine)
1 tsp salt
Filling:
9 oz shallots
2 tbs butter
7 oz Roquefort cheese
2/3 cup crème fraîche
2 eggs
Salt & pepper to taste

Prep time: 70 minutes
Per serving: 550 calories
14 g protein / 39 g fat / 33 g
carbohydrates

1 Put the flour in a bowl. Cut the butter into small pieces and add it to the bowl with 3 tbs of the wine and the salt. With a fork, work the ingredients until the mixture resembles coarse meal, adding more wine if necessary. Dump the mixture onto a work surface and knead slightly until the mixture holds together (take care not to overwork the dough). Shape the dough into a disk and wrap with plastic wrap. Refrigerate for 30 minutes.

2 Let the dough soften for 5-10 minutes. Lightly dust a work surface with flour. Roll out the dough, starting from the center and moving to the edges, to an 11-inch circle, adding a sprinkling of flour when necessary to prevent sticking. Carefully transfer the dough to a 10-inch pan. With your fingers, smooth any wrinkles in the dough. Trim the dough edges even with the pan. Refrigerate until ready to use.

3 Preheat the oven to 400°F. Peel and finely slice the shallots. Heat the butter in a skillet over low heat. Add the shallots and sauté for 10 minutes, until soft. Remove the skillet from the heat and let the shallots cool.

4 Cut the Roquefort into small pieces and put them in a bowl with the crème fraîche. Add the eggs and blend well. Mix in the shallots and season with salt and pepper.

5 Distribute the cheese-shallot mixture evenly in the crust. Bake until the filling is set and the crust is golden brown, about 30 minutes.

Smoked Salmon and Leek Quiche

● good for guests
● sophisticated

Serves 6
Rich Pastry 1, page 6
28 oz leeks
7 oz sliced smoked salmon
1 cup crème fraîche
2 eggs
Salt & pepper to taste
Pinch of cayenne pepper

Prep time: 75 minutes
Per serving: 470 calories
14 g protein / 31 g fat / 35 g
carbohydrates

1 Make the pastry and use it to line a 10-inch pan. Refrigerate until ready to use.

2 Preheat the oven to 400°F. Cut the leeks in half lengthwise and wash thoroughly. Cut the leeks into small half-rings. Bring a large pot of salted water to a boil. Add the leeks and boil for 1 minute. Drain, plunge the leeks into ice water, and drain again well.

3 Cut the smoked salmon into narrow strips and put them in a bowl with the leeks. In another bowl, mix the crème fraîche and eggs, and season with salt, pepper, and cayenne. Mix with the salmon-leek mixture.

4 Distribute the leek-salmon mixture evenly in the crust. Bake until the filling is set and the crust is golden brown, about 30 minutes.

Tip! Make this into mini-quiches, and serve them with a mixed green salad for a perfect luncheon dish.

Tomato Quiche with Herbed Cheese

● sophisticated
● vegetarian

Serves 6
Rich Pastry 2:
1 2/3 cups flour
4 oz cold butter
About 2 tbs water
1 egg
1 tsp salt
Filling:
26 oz tomatoes
1 bunch fresh basil
2/3 cup heavy cream
10 oz herbed cheese
   spread, such as Boursin
2 eggs
Salt & pepper to taste

Prep time: 65 minutes
Per serving: 570 calories
12 g protein / 41 g fat / 40 g
carbohydrates

1 Put the flour in a bowl. Cut the butter into small pieces; add it to the bowl with the water, egg, and salt. With a fork, work the mixture until it resembles coarse meal, adding a few more drops of water if necessary. Dump the mixture onto a work surface and knead slightly just until the mixture holds together. Shape the dough into a disk and wrap with plastic wrap. Refrigerate the dough for 30 minutes.

2 Let the dough soften for 5-10 minutes. Lightly dust a work surface with flour. Roll out the dough, starting from the center and moving to the edges, to an 11-inch circle, adding a sprinkling of flour when necessary to prevent sticking. Carefully transfer the dough to a 10-inch pan, centering it. With your fingers, smooth any wrinkles. Trim the dough edges even with the pan. Refrigerate until ready to use.

3 Preheat the oven to 400°F. Briefly plunge the tomatoes into boiling water to loosen the skins. Remove the skins and cut the tomatoes into eighths. Rinse the basil, strip the leaves, and chop them into narrow strips.

4 In a bowl, blend the heavy cream with the herbed cheese. Blend in the eggs. Season with salt and pepper, and stir in the basil.

5 Arrange the tomatoes in the crust, season with salt and pepper, and pour over the egg mixture. Bake until the filling is set and the crust is golden brown, about 35 minutes.

Shrimp Quiche with Saffron

● sophisticated
● easy

Serves 6
Basic Pastry, page 9
9 oz cooked and peeled
  shrimp
2 tbs fresh lemon juice
1/2 bunch fresh dill
2 shallots
1 tbs butter
2 eggs
1/8 tsp ground saffron
Salt & white pepper to
  taste
1 cup heavy cream

Prep time: 60 minutes
Per serving: 450 calories
16 g protein / 29 g fat / 30 g
carbohydrates

1 Make the pastry dough
and use it to line a 10-
inch pan. Refrigerate
until ready to use.

2 Rinse the shrimp in
cold water and pat dry.
Put the shrimp in a bowl
and drizzle with the
lemon juice. Wash the
dill, strip the leaves, and
finely chop them. Mix the
dill with the shrimp.
Cover the bowl with
plastic wrap and
refrigerate until ready
to use.

3 Preheat the oven to
400°F. Peel and finely
chop the shallots. Melt
the butter in a skillet over
medium heat and sauté
the shallots until soft,
about 5 minutes. Remove
from the heat and cool.

4 Break the eggs into a
bowl. Stir in the saffron
and season the eggs with
salt and pepper. Stir in
the cream.

5 Distribute the shrimp
in the crust and pour the
egg filling evenly on top.
Bake the quiche until the
filling is set and the crust
is golden brown, about
30 minutes.

Smoked Trout Quiche

● easy
● good for guests

Serves 6
Cream Cheese Pastry,
  page 6
12 oz smoked trout fillets
1 1/3 cups crème fraîche
2 tbs prepared horseradish
1 tbs fresh lemon juice
1 bunch fresh chives
Salt & white pepper to
  taste
2 eggs

Prep time: 70 minutes
Per serving: 610 calories
22 g protein / 48 g fat / 23 g
carbohydrates

1 Make the pastry and
use it to line a 10-inch
pan. Refrigerate until
ready to use.

2 Preheat the oven to
400°F. In a blender or
food processor, puree the
trout fillets with the
crème fraîche. Mix in the
horseradish and the
lemon juice. Wash and
finely chop the chives,
then stir them into the
puree. Season with salt
and pepper.

3 Separate the eggs and
blend the yolks into the
trout mixture.

4 In a clean, oil-free
bowl, beat the whites into
stiff peaks and fold them
into the egg yolk mixture
evenly.

5 Distribute the trout
filling evenly in the crust
and bake the quiche until
the filling is set and the
crust is golden brown,
about 35 minutes.

above: Smoked Trout
Quiche
below: Shrimp Quiche with
Saffron

Gorgonzola Quiche with Pears

- sophisticated
- good for guests

Serves 6
2 medium-sized ripe pears
5 tbs fresh lemon juice
7 oz Gorgonzola cheese
8 oz mascarpone cheese
2 eggs
Salt & pepper to taste
Pinch of freshly grated
   nutmeg
1 sheet frozen puff pastry
   (half of one 17.3-oz
   package), thawed

Prep time: 60 minutes
Per serving: 510 calories
16 g protein / 36 g fat / 34 g
carbohydrates

1 Peel the pears, halve lengthwise, and core. Drizzle the fruit with the lemon juice, put in a saucepan, and cover (barely) with water. Bring the water to a boil, cover, and cook over low heat for 5 minutes. Lift out the pears and drain well.

2 In a bowl, crush the Gorgonzola using a fork. Mix in the mascarpone and eggs and season with salt, pepper, and nutmeg.

3 Preheat the oven to 425°F. Lightly dust a work surface with flour. With a rolling pin, roll out the puff pastry, starting from the center and moving to the edges, trying to nudge the dough into an approximate 11-inch circle. Add a sprinkling of flour if necessary to prevent sticking. Carefully transfer the dough to a 10-inch pan. With your fingers, smooth any wrinkles. Trim the dough edges even with the pan.

4 Cut the pear halves crosswise into thin strips. Arrange the pears in the crust and pour the cheese filling in between the segments. Bake for 10 minutes. Reduce the oven heat to 400°F and bake until the filling is set and the crust is golden brown, about 20 minutes.

Smoked Fish & Fennel Quiche

● sophisticated
● make ahead

Serves 6
Cream Cheese Pastry,
   page 6
About 1 lb fresh fennel
Salt
14 oz smoked fish fillets
2 eggs
1 cup milk
Salt & pepper to taste
Freshly grated nutmeg to
   taste

Prep time: 65 minutes
Per serving: 460 calories
24 g protein / 29 g fat / 27 g
carbohydrates

the chopped fennel fronds, and season with salt and pepper. Lay the smoked fish on top of the fennel and pour the egg-milk mixture over the top. Bake until the filling is set and the crust is golden brown, about 35 minutes.

Tip! Use your favorite type of smoked fish, such as trout, salmon, or sturgeon.

1 Make the pastry and use it to line a 10-inch pan. Refrigerate until ready to use.

2 Preheat the oven to 400°F. Trim and wash the fennel. Cut off the green fronds, finely chop, and set aside. Finely slice the fennel bulbs lengthwise. Cook the fennel in boiling salted water until just firm to the bite, about 3 minutes, and drain well.

3 Slice the smoked fish fillets diagonally into 1/4-inch strips. Whisk the eggs with the milk and season generously with salt, pepper, and nutmeg.

4 Distribute the fennel in the crust, sprinkle with

In this chapter you'll find recipes for hearty quiches and tarts that serve as a complete meal for 4 people. If you plan on serving soup or an appetizer first, and maybe dessert, too, these recipes will serve 6 people. Complement the quiche with a sauce (tips and recipes on pages 28 and 29) or a crisp salad.

Stylish Salads

The following side salads go with nearly any quiche. You can find the ingredients year-round, so you can combine things without worrying about whether or not they are in season. Each salad serves 4-6 as a side dish. Treat the vinaigrette dressing as a base recipe and vary it as much as you please.

Mixed Salad with Chive Vinaigrette
1 head leaf lettuce
9 oz tomatoes
1 small cucumber
1 yellow bell pepper

Chive vinaigrette:

1 bunch fresh chives
2 tbs wine vinegar
Salt & pepper to taste
1 tsp mustard
5 tbs canola oil

Trim, wash and dry the lettuce, and tear the leaves into bite-sized pieces. Wash the tomatoes, cut into wedges, and core. Peel, quarter, and slice the cucumber into thick pieces. Trim and wash the bell pepper, cut lengthwise into eighths, then slice into narrow strips. For the vinaigrette: Wash the chives and finely chop. In a large salad bowl, mix the vinegar, salt, pepper, and mustard. Then, using a whisk, blend in the oil gradually until you have a creamy mixture. Toss all salad ingredients well in the vinaigrette and serve with quiche.

Hearty Offerings

Tomato Salad with Green Onions

Wash 20 oz tomatoes, slice, and layer them overlapping on a plate. Season with salt and pepper. Trim and wash 3 green onions, finely chop them, and scatter them over the tomatoes. Drizzle with the Chive Vinaigrette (p 16).

Romaine Salad with Radishes

Cut 1 head of romaine into broad strips, wash, and dry well. Trim and wash 1 bunch of radishes, and cut each radish into quarters. Wash and dry a handful of radish sprouts. Toss all ingredients well with the Chive Vinaigrette (p 16).

Cucumber Salad with Dill and Sesame

Peel a large cucumber and cut it into slices. Into the Chive Vinaigrette (p 16) mix 1/4 cup plain yogurt and 1/2 bunch of dill, chopped. In a nonstick skillet, toast 2 tbs sesame seeds until golden brown and mix with the other ingredients. Pour the dressing over the sliced cucumber and toss.

Vinaigrette variations:

You can play with the vinaigrette recipe on page 16 by omitting the chives and adding one of the following ingredients:
- 1/4 cup plain yogurt
- 4 oz crumbled blue cheese
- 4 oz crumbled feta cheese
- 4 oz crumbled bacon
- 1 shallot, finely chopped
- 2 cloves garlic, minced

A fresh, sweet finish

After a rich savory quiche, spoil yourself and your guests with a light dessert. A bowl of fresh fragrant seasonal fruits, such as sweet ripe strawberries or cherries, is always nicer and more refreshing after a quiche than a rich, heavy finale. No matter what the season, a selection of ripe fruits is a great idea.

The fruit salad recipe below serves 4 to 6 as a dessert. Lightly whipped cream flavored with a hint of sugar and vanilla, or even vanilla ice cream, are good compliments.

Summer Fruit Salad

Quarter a ripe, fragrant melon (such as a cantaloupe), remove the seeds, and cut the flesh into small cubes. Mix the melon in a bowl with 8 oz washed, trimmed, and sliced strawberries and 6 oz washed blueberries. Mix 1/4 cup honey with 1/4 cup lemon juice and maybe 2 tbs chopped green pistachios and pour over the fruit salad. Garnish with fresh mint (optional). Cover the bowl with plastic wrap and refrigerate for 30 minutes before serving.

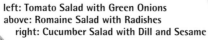

left: Tomato Salad with Green Onions
above: Romaine Salad with Radishes
right: Cucumber Salad with Dill and Sesame

Corned Beef & Cabbage Quiche

● inexpensive
● make ahead

Serves 4
Rich Pastry 1, page 6
1 head green cabbage
  (about 28 oz)
1 large onion
1 lb cooked corned beef
1 tbs canola oil
Salt & pepper to taste
1 tbs caraway seeds
3 eggs
2/3 cup crème fraîche

Prep time: 70 minutes
Per serving: 1000 calories
32 g protein / 77 g fat / 50 g
carbohydrates

1 Make the pastry and use it to line a 10-inch pan. Refrigerate until ready to use.

2 Preheat the oven to 400°F. Quarter the cabbage, cut out the core, and cut each quarter into fine strips. Wash the cabbage strips and drain well.

3 Peel and finely chop the onion. Cut the corned beef into dice. In a wide skillet, heat the oil and sauté the onion until translucent. Add the corned beef and sauté briefly. Mix in the cabbage and sauté for 15 minutes. Season with salt, pepper, and caraway seeds. Remove the pan from the heat and cool.

4 Stir together the eggs and crème fraîche. Add to the cabbage-corned beef mixture and distribute in the crust. Bake until the filling is set and the crust is golden brown, about 40 minutes.

Smoked Sausage Quiche

● easy
● inexpensive

Serves 4
Rich Pastry 2, page 11
1 bunch green onions
2 tbs butter
1 lb smoked sausage,
  casings removed
1/2 cup heavy cream
3 tbs Dijon-style mustard
2 eggs
Salt & pepper to taste
2 oz Gouda cheese, freshly
  grated

Prep time: 60 minutes
Per serving: 1190 calories
30 g protein / 95 g fat / 53 g
carbohydrates

1 Make the pastry and use it to line a 10-inch pan. Refrigerate until ready to use.

2 Preheat the oven to 400°F. Trim and wash the green onions, and finely chop. In a skillet, heat the butter over medium heat, and sauté the onions for 5 minutes; cool.

3 Cut the sausage into medium slices. In a bowl, blend the cream with the mustard and eggs, season with salt and pepper, and mix in the green onions.

4 Layer overlapping slices of sausage in the crust. Pour the egg mixture on top and sprinkle with the cheese. Bake the quiche until the filling is set and the crust is golden brown, about 35 minutes.

Serving suggestion: Try this with Tomato Salad with Green Onions, page 17, or Tomato Sauce with Capers, page 29.

above: Corned Beef &
Cabbage Quiche
below: Smoked Sausage
Quiche

Broccoli Quiche with Turkey Breast

● make ahead
● good for guests

Serves 4
Basic Pastry, page 9
18 oz broccoli
8 oz fairly thick slices of
  smoked turkey breast
2 medium onions
1 tbs canola oil
10 oz sour cream
2 eggs
2 oz Gouda cheese, freshly
  grated
Salt & pepper to taste
Pinch of ground nutmeg

Prep time: 65 minutes
Per serving: 690 calories
29 g protein / 43 g fat / 51 g
carbohydrates

1 Make the pastry and use it to line a 10-inch pan. Refrigerate until ready to use.

2 Preheat the oven to 400°F. Divide the broccoli into small florets and wash. Peel the broccoli stalks, wash, and finely dice. Cook all of the broccoli in boiling water for 3 minutes. Drain, plunge into ice water, and drain again. Slice the turkey breast into narrow strips.

3 Peel and dice the onions. In a skillet, heat the oil over medium heat and sauté the onions until soft. Add the turkey, sauté briefly, and remove from the heat.

4 In a bowl, blend the sour cream with the eggs and cheese. Mix with the turkey-onion mixture, and season with salt, pepper, and nutmeg.

5 Distribute the broccoli in the crust and distribute the turkey-onion mixture on top. Pour the egg mixture evenly over the top. Bake the quiche until the filling is set and the crust is golden brown, about 35 minutes.

Serving suggestion: This is good with Gorgonzola Sauce, page 29.

Chili Pie

● easy
● sophisticated

Serves 4
Basic Pastry, page 9
2 cans kidney beans
  (about 9 oz each)
1 medium-sized leek
1 tbs olive oil
16 oz ground beef
5 tbs tomato paste
2 cloves garlic
Salt & pepper to taste
Pinch of chili powder
1 tsp dried oregano
1 egg
4 oz Monterey Jack
  cheese, freshly grated

Prep time: 60 minutes
Per serving: 780 calories
27 g protein / 24 g fat / 128 g
carbohydrates

1 Make the pastry and use it to line a 10-inch pan. Refrigerate until ready to use.

2 Preheat the oven to 400°F. Drain the kidney beans in a colander. Trim the leek, slit it lengthwise, wash it well, then thinly slice. In a large skillet, heat the oil over medium-high heat. Add the ground beef and sauté until crumbly, about 5 minutes. Add the leek and sauté for another 5 minutes. Mix in the tomato paste. Peel and mince the garlic, and stir it into the meat mixture.

3 Mix the beans in with the meat mixture and season generously with salt, pepper, chili powder, and oregano. Remove the pan from the heat and let the mixture cool.

4 In a large bowl, beat the egg with half of the cheese. Add the chili mixture, distribute evenly in the crust, and spread the top smooth. Scatter the remaining cheese on top and bake until the filling is set and the crust is golden brown, about 30 minutes.

Serving suggestion:
Accompany with a tomato-bell pepper salad or Spicy Red Pepper Sauce, page 29.

Pork Tenderloin Quiche

● sophisticated
● easy

Serves 4
Rich Pastry 2, page 11,
  substituting half whole-
  wheat flour
16 oz pork tenderloin
2 cloves garlic
2 tbs canola oil
Salt & pepper to taste
Pinch of freshly grated
  nutmeg
3 tsp curry powder
10 oz frozen peas
3 eggs
1 cup milk

Prep time: 60 minutes
Per serving: 830 calories
40 g protein / 49 g fat / 61 g
carbohydrates

1 Make the pastry and
use it to line a 10-inch
pan. Refrigerate until
ready to use.

2 Preheat the oven to
400°F. Slice the pork into
narrow strips. Peel and
mince the garlic. In a
wide skillet, heat the oil
over medium heat. Add
the pork strips and garlic
and sauté for about 3
minutes. Season
generously with salt and
pepper. Stir in the
nutmeg and curry
powder. Remove the pan
from the heat.

3 Cook the peas in
boiling salted water for 3
minutes. Drain, plunge

the peas into ice water,
and drain well.

4 In a bowl, whisk the
eggs and milk well.
Season with salt, pepper,
and nutmeg.

5 Mix the peas with the
pork strips and distribute
in the crust. Pour the
egg-milk mixture on top
and bake until the filling
is set and the crust is
golden brown, about 30
minutes.

Serving suggestion:
Accent this with Herb
Yogurt Sauce, page 28, or
Spicy Red Pepper Sauce,
page 29.

Cheeseburger Quiche

○ inexpensive
● make ahead

Serves 4
Cream Cheese Pastry,
  page 6
1 large onion
2 tbs olive oil
2 cloves garlic
16 oz ground beef
5 tbs tomato paste
Salt & pepper to taste
1 tsp dried oregano
1 tsp dried thyme
1 bunch fresh Italian
  parsley
2 eggs
3 oz cheddar cheese,
  freshly grated

Prep time: 60 minutes
Per serving: 900 calories
22 g protein / 50 fat / 108 g
carbohydrates

1 Make the pastry and
use it to line a 10-inch
pan. Refrigerate until
ready to use.

2 Preheat the oven to
400°F. Peel and dice the
onion. In a large skillet,
heat the oil over medium
heat and sauté the onion
for 5 minutes. Peel and
mince the garlic and add
it to the pan.

3 Add the ground beef to
the onion-garlic mixture
and sauté until crumbly
and no pink remains,
about 10 minutes. Blend
in the tomato paste and
season with salt, pepper,
oregano, and thyme.

Remove the pan from the
heat and cool slightly.

4 Wash the parsley, then
strip and finely chop the
leaves. In a bowl, mix the
parsley with the eggs and
half of the cheese. Mix
with the beef mixture.

5 Distribute the ground
beef-egg mixture in the
crust, spread the top
smooth, and sprinkle with
the remaining cheese.
Bake the quiche until the
filling is set and the crust
is golden brown, about
30 minutes.

Serving suggestion:
Serve with Gorgonzola
Sauce or Spicy Red
Pepper Sauce, page 29,
and your favorite salad.

Variation

For a vegetarian version, use a rice filling as a base: Simmer 1 cup long-grain rice in 2 cups salted water for 20 minutes. Cool. Trim, wash and finely chop 1 large leek. Finely dice 7 oz carrots and sauté with the leek in 1 tbs butter for 3 minutes. Mix 3 1/2 oz freshly grated Parmesan cheese with the vegetables and season with salt, pepper, and nutmeg. Whisk together 3 eggs and 1 1/3 cups heavy cream, and blend with the rice. Distribute the rice filling in the crust and bake at 350°F for about 50 minutes.

above: Cheeseburger Quiche
below: Pork Tenderloin Quiche

Meat Loaf &
Cabbage Quiche

- inexpensive
- make ahead

Serves 4
Rich Pastry 2, page 11
1 large onion
2 tbs canola oil
1 small Savoy cabbage
    (about 24 oz)
6 tsp dry white wine (or
    chicken stock)
Salt & pepper to taste
1/2 tsp ground caraway
    seeds
8 oz meat loaf
2 eggs
1 1/4 cups sour cream
Pinch of ground nutmeg
2 oz Havarti cheese,
    freshly grated

Prep time: 75 minutes
Per serving: 890 calories
26 g protein / 52 g fat / 81 g
carbohydrates

1 Make the pastry and use it to line a 10-inch pan. Refrigerate until ready to use.

2 Preheat the oven to 400°F. Peel and dice the onion. In a large skillet, heat the oil over medium heat and sauté the onion until translucent.

3 Trim, quarter, and core the cabbage. Wash the cabbage and slice into narrow strips. Add the cabbage to the skillet and sauté for 5 minutes. Add the white wine, season with salt, pepper, and caraway seeds, and sauté for 5 more minutes. Remove from the heat and let cool.

4 Cube the meat loaf and mix with the cabbage mixture. In a bowl, whisk the eggs with the sour cream and season generously with salt, pepper, and nutmeg.

5 Distribute the cabbage-meat mixture evenly in the crust. Pour the egg mixture over the top and sprinkle with the cheese. Bake until the filling is set and the crust is golden brown, about 30 minutes.

Serving suggestion: This is delicious accompanied by Tomato Sauce with Capers, page 29.

Chicken Liver Quiche

● sophisticated
● easy

Serves 4
Basic Pastry, page 9
2 onions
3 cloves garlic
16 oz chicken livers
3 tbs canola oil
Salt & pepper to taste
1 tsp dried oregano
1 bunch fresh basil
2/3 cup crème fraîche
9 oz pureed tomatoes
   (canned)
2 eggs
1 tsp hot paprika

Prep time: 70 minutes
Per serving: 700 calories
36 g protein / 38 g fat / 56 g
carbohydrates

1 Make the pastry and use it to line a 10-inch pan. Refrigerate until ready to use.

2 Peel and dice the onions. Peel and mince the garlic. Remove the skins and sinews from the chicken livers; briefly rinse with cold water, pat dry, and separate the livers into their natural segments.

3 In a large skillet, heat 2 tbs of the oil over medium heat and sauté the livers for 5 minutes; transfer the livers to a plate. Sauté the onions in the remaining 1 tbs oil until soft. Add the garlic and livers, sauté briefly, and season with salt, pepper, and oregano.

4 Wash the basil, then strip the leaves cut them into thin strips. In a bowl, blend the crème fraîche with the pureed tomatoes and eggs. Stir in the basil and season generously with salt, pepper, and the paprika.

5 Distribute the chicken liver mixture in the crust and pour the tomato-egg mixture on top. Bake until the filling is set and the crust is golden brown, about 30 minutes.

Paté & Apple Tart

- ○ easy
- ● good for guests

Serves 4
Cream Cheese Pastry,
    page 6
1 bunch green onions
2 small apples (about
    10 oz), such as Gala,
    McIntosh, or Golden
    Delicious)
2 tbs fresh lemon juice
2 tbs butter
Salt & pepper to taste
1 tsp dried marjoram
14 oz country-style paté

Prep time: 60 minutes
Per serving: 880 calories
24 g protein / 68 g fat / 45 g
carbohydrates

1 Make the pastry and use it to line a 10-inch pan. Refrigerate until ready to use.

2 Preheat the oven to 400°F. Wash and finely chop the green onions. Peel the apples, cut them into eighths, then cut each section in half. Drizzle the apples with the lemon juice.

3 In a large skillet, melt the butter over medium heat. Add the green onions and apple wedges and sauté for 5 minutes. Season with salt, pepper, and marjoram.

4 Crumble the paté, add it to the pan, and sauté for 5 minutes. Remove the pan from the heat.

5 Distribute the paté mixture evenly in the crust and bake the tart until golden brown, about 30 minutes.

Serving suggestion:
Serve with Mixed Salad with Chive Vinaigrette, page 16.

Variation
Instead of paté use 14 oz liverwurst.
For a vegetarian version, dice 20 oz potatoes, sauté for 10 minutes in 3 tbs butter with one diced onion, season with salt and pepper, then mix in the apples.

Tip! This quiche freezes well and also tastes good when served at room temperature. It's ideal for a buffet or picnic. Note: never freeze a quiche for longer than 3 months. The less time spent in the freezer, the better the quality. Look for other practical tips on page 41.

Vegetarian Selections

These days more and more people are replacing the meat in their diet with vegetables and salads. The range of creative, delicious vegetarian dishes is huge—including vegetable quiches and tarts. Different kinds of vegetables can be mixed and matched in fillings. Some vegetable quiches taste best solo, others are best paired with a sauce.

Scrumptious sauces

While the quiche is baking in the oven you can prepare the sauce. Any leftover sauce will keep covered in the refrigerator for about 3 days. The Herb-Yogurt Sauce and the Feta Sauce with Olives also make great dips for cooked and raw vegetables; the hot sauces are a natural with pasta. The Spicy Red Pepper Sauce is an ideal dip for tacos or other finger foods.

The following sauces go with many different kinds of quiche and serve 4-6.

Herb-Yogurt Sauce
1 1/4 cups crème fraîche
12 oz plain yogurt
5 tbs fresh lemon juice
1 tsp mustard
Salt & pepper to taste
3 cloves garlic
2 shallots
1 bunch fresh Italian
  parsley
1 bunch fresh chives
1 bunch fresh basil
1/2 bunch fresh dill

Pour the crème fraîche and yogurt into a bowl. Blend with the lemon juice and mustard, and season with salt and pepper. Peel and mince the garlic and add it to the bowl. Peel and finely chop the shallots and add to the bowl. Wash the herbs, finely chop, stir into the sauce and season to taste.

Tomato Sauce with Capers

1 onion
2 tbs olive oil
2 cloves garlic
2 1/4 lb large tomatoes (or one 14 1/2-oz can of tomatoes)
1 tsp dried thyme
1 tsp dried oregano
Salt & pepper to taste
3 tbs drained capers

Peel and dice the onion. In a skillet, heat the olive oil over medium heat and sauté the onion until soft. Peel and mince the garlic and add it to the pan.

Briefly plunge the tomatoes into boiling water to loosen the skins. Remove the skins and seeds, chop the tomatoes, and add to the skillet. Season with thyme, oregano, salt and pepper. Simmer for 20 minutes, then mix in the capers and season to taste.

Gorgonzola Sauce

1 1/3 cups heavy cream
8 oz Gorgonzola cheese
Salt & pepper to taste
1 bunch fresh Italian parsley, or 2 oz walnut halves

In a saucepan, heat the cream. With a fork, crush the Gorgonzola and add it to the pan, blending with the cream. Simmer for 15 minutes, stirring continuously, until the cheese has completely melted. Season with salt and pepper. Meanwhile, wash the parsley, strip and finely chop the leaves (or finely chop the walnuts). Your choice: mix in the parsley or walnuts.

Feta Sauce with Olives

7 oz Greek feta (sheep's-milk cheese)
10 oz plain yogurt
2 cloves garlic
2 oz kalamata olives, pitted
2 tbs fresh lemon juice
Salt & pepper to taste

Put the feta and yogurt in a bowl and blend with a mixer. Peel and mince the garlic and add it to the bowl. Stir in the olives and season the sauce with the lemon juice, salt, and pepper.

Spicy Red Pepper Sauce

3 red bell peppers
4 cloves garlic
1 fresh red chile
3 tbs olive oil
1 tbs fresh lemon juice
Salt & pepper to taste
1 tsp hot paprika

Preheat the broiler. Trim the bell peppers, quarter them lengthwise, and wash. Line a baking sheet with aluminum foil and lay the pepper slices on top, skin-side up. Broil until the pepper skin blackens and blisters, about 10 minutes. Peel the garlic, and remove the seeds from the chile. Peel the roasted bell peppers and puree in a blender or food processor with the garlic and chile. Mix in the oil and lemon juice, and season with salt, pepper, and paprika.

Zucchini Mini-Quiches

○ inexpensive
● good for guests

Serves 6
Cream Cheese Pastry,
  page 6
2 tsp dried oregano
1 3/4 lb zucchini
Salt
1 cup plain yogurt
2 eggs
2 oz Parmesan cheese,
  freshly grated
1 bunch fresh basil
2 cloves garlic
Salt & pepper to taste
3 tbs sesame seeds

Prep time: 70 minutes
Per serving: 410 calories
22 g protein / 25 g fat / 29 g
carbohydrates

1 Make the pastry, adding the dried oregano with the salt. Refrigerate for 30 minutes.

2 Wash and trim the zucchini, and cut into thin diagonal slices (a mandoline or vegetable slicer is helpful). Cook the zucchini in boiling salted water for 1 minute and drain well.

3 Blend the yogurt with the eggs and half of the Parmesan. Wash the basil, strip the leaves, finely chop them, and add them to the yogurt mixture. Peel and mice the garlic, and add to the mixture. Season generously with salt and pepper.

4 Let the dough soften at room temperature for 5-10 minutes. Lightly dust a work surface with flour. With a rolling pin, roll out the dough, starting from the center and moving to the edges, until it is about 1/8-inch thick. With a large round dough cutter, or inverted jar or drinking glass, cut out six 5-inch circles, adding a sprinkling of flour when necessary to prevent sticking. Carefully transfer the circles to 4-inch pans, smoothing any wrinkles. Trim the dough edges even with the pans.

5 Preheat the oven to 400°F. Distribute the yogurt mixture evenly in each crust. Layer the zucchini slices, overlapping, on top.

6 Mix the sesame seeds with the remaining Parmesan and scatter evenly on top of the zucchini. Bake until the filling is set and the crust is golden brown, about 40 minutes.

Serving suggestion:
Tastes great accompanied by Tomato Sauce with Capers, page 29.

Mushroom Quiche with Snow Peas

● good for guests
● sophisticated

Serves 4
Cream Cheese Pastry,
  page 6
9 oz snow peas
Salt
1 lb oyster mushrooms
2 tbs olive oil
2 cloves garlic
Salt & pepper to taste
3 oz Gorgonzola cheese
2 oz mascarpone cheese
2 eggs

Prep time: 75 minutes
Per serving: 710 calories
23 g protein / 52 g fat / 42 g
carbohydrates

1 Make the pastry and use it to line a 10-inch pan. Refrigerate until ready to use.

2 Preheat the oven to 400°F. Trim and wash the snow peas, and remove the strings. Cook the peas in boiling salted water for about 2 minutes. Drain, plunge into ice water, and drain well.

3 Clean the oyster mushrooms and cut into broad strips. In a skillet, heat the oil over medium-high heat and sauté the mushrooms for 5 minutes. Peel and mince the garlic, add it to the pan, sauté briefly, and season the mixture with salt and pepper. Remove from the heat.

4 In a blender or food processor, puree half of the peas with the Gorgonzola and mascarpone. Season the puree to taste with salt and pepper, and blend in the eggs.

5 Distribute the oyster mushrooms and remaining peas in the crust. Pour the egg mixture on top and bake until the filling is set and the crust is golden brown, about 45 minutes.

Curried Cauliflower Quiche

○ inexpensive
● sophisticated

Serves 4
Rich Pastry 1, page 6
1 cauliflower (about
** 2 1/4 lb)**
Salt
1 bunch green onions
1 tbs butter
8 oz cream cheese,
** softened**
1 cup plain yogurt
2 eggs
Heaping tbs curry powder
2 tbs ground almonds
Salt & pepper to taste
2 tbs fresh lemon juice

Prep time: 80 minutes
Per serving: 690 calories
29 g protein / 43 g fat / 58 g
carbohydrates

1 Make the pastry and use it to line a 10-inch pan. Refrigerate until ready to use.

2 Preheat the oven to 400°F. Wash the cauliflower, divide it into small florets, and cook in boiling salted water for no more than 5 minutes; drain well.

3 Trim, wash, and finely chop the green onions. In a skillet, heat the butter over medium heat. Sauté the green onion in the butter for 3 minutes.

4 Blend the cream cheese and yogurt with the eggs, curry, and almonds. Season to taste with salt, pepper, and lemon juice. Mix in the sautéed green onions.

5 Distribute the cauliflower in the crust, and pour the cream cheese mixture evenly over the top. Bake until the filling is set and the crust is golden brown, about 45 minutes.

Eggplant Tart with Mozzarella

● good for guests
● make ahead

Serves 4
Rich Pastry 2, page 11
3 tsp dried thyme
20 oz eggplant
6 tbs olive oil
3 cloves garlic
1 tsp dried oregano
Salt & pepper to taste
18 oz large tomatoes
8 oz fresh Mozzarella
  cheese

Prep time: 75 minutes
Per serving: 830 calories
24 g protein / 54 g fat / 64 g
carbohydrates

1 Make the pastry, adding 2 tsp of the thyme with the salt. Use the pastry to line a 10-inch pan. Refrigerate it until ready to use.

2 Preheat the oven to 400°F. Wash the eggplant, remove the stems, and cut into fairly thick slices. In a large skillet, heat 4 tbs of the oil over high heat and sauté the eggplant until golden brown on both sides. Peel and mince the garlic, and add it to the pan with the remaining 1 tsp thyme, the oregano, salt, and pepper. Remove the eggplant from the pan and remove the pan from the heat.

3 Briefly plunge the tomatoes into boiling water to loosen the skins. Remove the skins and cut the tomatoes into thick slices. Cut the mozzarella into thick slices.

4 Alternate overlapping layers of eggplant, tomato, and mozzarella slices in the crust. Season with salt and pepper and drizzle with the remaining 2 tbs olive oil. Bake the tart until golden brown, about 40 minutes.

Serving suggestion:
Accompany with Herb Yogurt Sauce, page 29.

Carrot & Broccoli Quiche

- inexpensive
- easy

Serves 4
Rich Pastry 1, page 6
12 oz carrots
Salt
18 oz broccoli
2 oz pine nuts
Salt & pepper to taste
Pinch of cayenne pepper
Pinch of ground cumin
8 oz sour cream
3 eggs

Prep time: 60 minutes
Per serving: 650 calories
19 g protein / 41 g fat / 57 g
carbohydrates

1 Make the pastry and use it to line a 10-inch pan. Refrigerate until ready to use.

2 Preheat the oven to 400°F. Peel the carrots and slice them thinly. Cook the carrots in a large pot of boiling salted water for 4 minutes. Drain, plunge into ice water, and drain well.

3 Divide the broccoli into small florets, setting aside the stalks for another use. Cook the broccoli florets in boiling salted water for 3 minutes. Drain, plunge into ice water, and drain again. In a dry nonstick skillet, toast the pine nuts until golden brown.

4 Distribute the broccoli and carrots in the crust. Sprinkle with the pine nuts. Season everything with salt, pepper, cayenne, and cumin.

5 In a bowl, blend the sour cream with the eggs, season generously with salt and pepper, and pour the mixture on top of the carrots and broccoli. Bake until the filling is set and the crust is golden brown, about 30 minutes.

Variations
Leeks and zucchini are both excellent substitutes for broccoli. The quiche will also be more substantial if you sprinkle 5 oz of diced salami, smoked bacon, or ham on top of the vegetables. You can also mix 4 oz of your favorite grated cheese in with the sour cream.

Tip! You can find carrots anytime of year. In late May you'll start to see baby new carrots at your farmers' market or in supermarket produce bins. Tender baby carrots are typically sold by the bunch with their greens still attached. Carrots contain lots of carotene which our bodies convert to vitamin A. But for this to happen carrots need to be eaten together with fat, so even when eaten raw, they should always be served with a tad of butter, oil or cream—which also enhances their special flavor.

Spinach Quiche with Feta and Olives

○ takes a while
● sophisticated

Serves 4
Rich Pastry 2, page 11
28 oz fresh leaf spinach
  (or 20 oz frozen spinach)
Salt
2 onions
2 tbs olive oil
3 cloves garlic
Salt & pepper to taste
Pinch of ground nutmeg
5 oz feta cheese
2 eggs
1/2 cup milk
2 oz black olives, pitted

Prep time: 75 minutes
Per serving: 720 calories
22 g protein / 44 g fat / 60 g
carbohydrates

1 Make the pastry and use it to line a 10-inch pan. Refrigerate until ready to use.

2 Preheat the oven to 400°F. Wash the fresh spinach thoroughly. (Thaw frozen spinach.) Plunge the fresh spinach quickly into boiling salted water and drain well.

3 Peel and dice the onions. In a wide skillet, heat the olive oil over medium heat and sauté the onions until translucent. Peel and mince the garlic and add it to the pan. Mix in the

spinach, sauté briefly, and season with salt, pepper, and nutmeg.

4 In a bowl, crush the feta using a fork. Mix with the eggs and milk, and season the mixture with salt and pepper.

5 Distribute the spinach mixture in the crust and pour the egg mixture evenly over the top. Scatter the olives on top and bake the quiche until the filling is set and the crust is golden brown, about 30 minutes.

Red Lentil Quiche

● sophisticated
○ inexpensive

Serves 4
Cream Cheese Pastry,
  page 6
4 tsp curry powder
2 onions
2 cloves garlic
Walnut–sized piece of
  fresh ginger
2 tbs olive oil
9 oz dried red lentils
Salt & pepper to taste
Pinch of cayenne pepper
2 cups vegetable stock
2 large tomatoes (about
  14 oz)
1 cup milk
3 eggs

Prep time: 65 minutes
Per serving: 920 calories
38 g protein / 46 g fat / 93 g
carbohydrates

1 Make the pastry, adding 2 tsp of the curry powder with the salt. Use the pasty to line a 10-inch pan. Refrigerate until ready to use.

2 Preheat the oven to 400°F. Peel and dice the onions. Peel and mince the garlic and ginger. In a skillet, heat the oil over medium heat and sauté the onions until translucent. Add the garlic and ginger and sauté the mixture for another 3 minutes.

3 Add the lentils to the pan and season with salt, pepper, the remaining 2 tsp curry powder and the cayenne pepper. Pour in the vegetable stock, bring to a boil, cover, and simmer for 15 minutes. Let cool.

4 Core the tomatoes. Briefly plunge the tomatoes into boiling water to loosen the skins. Remove skins and seeds, and dice the tomatoes. In a bowl, whisk the milk with the eggs.

5 Mix the tomatoes in with the lentils, and distribute evenly in the crust. Pour the egg-milk filling on top. Bake until the filling is set and the crust is golden brown, about 35 minutes.

above: Spinach Quiche with Feta and Olives
below: Red Lentil Quiche

Shallot Quiche with Raisins

● sophisticated
● good for guests

Serves 4
Rich Pastry 2, page 11,
    substituting apple juice
    for the water
1 3/4 lb shallots
3 tbs olive oil
3 tbs raisins
3 tbs curry powder
Salt & pepper to taste
1/2 cup apple juice
2 oz slivered almonds
2 eggs
1 cup heavy cream
2 oz Parmesan cheese,
    freshly grated
Pinch of freshly grated
    nutmeg

Prep time: 70 minutes
Per serving: 970 calories
25 g protein / 58 g fat / 93 g
carbohydrates

1 Make the pastry and
use it to line a 10-inch
pan. Refrigerate until
ready to use.

2 Preheat the oven to
400°F. Peel the shallots
and chop them
lengthwise into narrow
strips. In a skillet, heat the
olive oil over medium
heat and sauté the
shallots and raisins until
shallots are translucent.

3 Season the shallot-
raisin mixture with the
curry powder, salt, and
pepper. Add the apple
juice, reduce the heat to
low, and simmer for 10
minutes. Remove from
the heat, stir in the
almond slivers, and cool.

4 In a bowl, mix the eggs,
cream, and Parmesan.
Season with salt, pepper,
and nutmeg.

5 Distribute the shallot-
raisin mixture in the crust
and pour the egg mixture
over the top. Bake until
the filling is set and the
crust is golden brown, 30
to 40 minutes.

Chinese Cabbage Quiche

● make ahead
● inexpensive

Serves 4
Rich Pastry 1, page 6
1 small head Chinese
    cabbage (about 18 oz)
1 clove garlic
Walnut-sized piece fresh
    ginger
2 tbs butter
Salt & pepper to taste
Pinch of cayenne pepper
1 tsp Chinese 5-spice
    powder
3 tbs soy sauce
1 bunch fresh cilantro (or
    Italian parsley)
9 oz firm tofu
2/3 cup crème fraîche
3 eggs

Prep time: 75 minutes
Per serving: 690 calories
19 g protein / 49 g fat / 45 g
carbohydrates

1 Make the pastry and
use it to line a 10-inch
pan. Refrigerate until
ready to use.

2 Preheat the oven to
400°F. Trim the cabbage,
slice it into narrow strips,
wash, and drain well. Peel
and mince the garlic and
the ginger.

3 In a large skillet, melt
the butter over medium
heat and briefly sauté the
ginger and garlic. Mix in
the cabbage and sauté
for 5 minutes. Season
generously with salt,
pepper, cayenne, 5-spice
powder, and soy sauce.
Wash the cilantro, strip
and finely chop the
leaves, and briefly sauté
with the other
ingredients. Remove the
pan from the heat; cool.

4 In a blender or food
processor, puree the tofu
with the crème fraîche.
Mix in the eggs, and
season with the salt
and pepper.

5 Mix the cabbage with
the tofu mixture and
distribute evenly in the
crust. Bake the quiche
until the filling is set and
the crust is golden brown,
about 40 minutes.

Fast and Practical Choices

Quiche is so versatile—you can serve quiche at an elegant dinner, at a casual Sunday brunch, as a snack, at a picnic, or as an appetizer with a glass of wine. And since quiche is so easy to make, it really pays off to stock the kitchen with quiche ingredients to feed those unexpected guests.

Prepared doughs—ready for filling

There are various ready-made doughs on the market, which you can roll out fast to make a quiche or tart crust.

Frozen puff pastry sheets

To speed things up, separate the dough pieces to thaw. Though it comes as a rectangle, puff pastry can be rolled out in a slightly circular shape to fit the pan. Trim the edges to fit. For a standard 10-inch round quiche, 1 sheet of dough is enough. However, you can easily make two quiches from the package of dough—eat one now and freeze one for later.

Chilled pizza or bread dough

Look for these in tubes near the dairy section in the supermarket. To use, remove the dough from the packaging, roll it out about 1/8-inch thick, and lay in the pan. A bonus—these doughs are much leaner than standard pastry doughs, perfect for calorie counters.

Refrigerated or frozen pie crust

Remove the crust from the packaging and carefully transfer it to the pan you wish to use. After trimming the sides, the crust is ready to be filled. Some brands of pie crust come already formed in an aluminum pan—perfect for spur-of-the-moment quiches.

Fresh from the pantry

In this chapter you'll find creative quiches and tarts made with ingredients you probably already have on hand. Refer to the short list of ingredients below, add eggs and milk or cream, and a few fresh herbs, and you can conjure up a quiche in an instant.

Basic Quiche Supplies:
- Canned garbanzo beans
- Canned or frozen corn
- Frozen Brussels sprouts and green beans
- Canned artichoke hearts
- Canned tuna
- Bacon
- Smoked sausage
- Lean ham, turkey breast, and chicken breast
- Various types of cheese
- Ready-made doughs

An elegant solution for leftovers

Wondering what to do with yesterday's cooked vegetables? Got sausage or roast from the weekend in the refrigerator? It's time to bake a quiche! Preheat the oven to 400°F. Chop some vegetables (your choice), mix with some leftover meat, poultry, sausage, or ham (diced or cut into thin strips) and distribute in the crust. Mix together 2-3 eggs (depending on how much filling you need), 1-1 1/3 cups heavy cream or milk, and 2-4 oz grated cheese, and pour into the crust. Bake for 30 minutes, until the filling is set and the crust is golden brown.

Practical tips for home-baked quiches

- You can create a delicious quiche a day in advance even without ready-made dough. Decide on your pastry dough and knead it. Clear a space in the refrigerator. Roll out the dough and make the crust. You can also prepare the ingredients in advance—chop everything you need and store them in containers.

It's important to then keep everything in the refrigerator. The next day just preheat the oven, distribute filling in the crust, pour the savory quiche custard on top— and that's it!
- You can keep leftover baked quiche for about 3 days in the refrigerator. Seal it well in aluminum foil or plastic wrap. Reheat the quiche at 400°F for 15 minutes until warm throughout.
- It's best to slice baked quiche before it goes into the freezer. Then you can take it out as you need it, for example, when unexpected company drops in, or if you're preparing in advance for a party. Put the frozen quiche in a preheated 400°F oven and bake for 25-30 minutes.

- If you plan to serve quiche as a hors d'oeuvre to go with cocktails, it's important to cut it up into small bite-sized pieces. Don't forget the napkins!
- If you're cooking for a crowd you can double all the recipes in this book and bake on a large rimmed baking sheet or broiler/baking pan. Cut the baked quiche into small pieces and keep it warm in a 150°F oven.

Make a delicious quiche with leftover vegetables— anything goes!

Tuna & Garbanzo Bean Quiche

● sophisticated
● make ahead

Serves 4
1 can water-packed tuna (6 oz)
1 can garbanzo beans (15 oz), drained
2 cloves garlic
1 tsp dried thyme
1 tsp dried oregano
Salt & pepper to taste
10 oz sour cream
2 eggs
2 oz Parmesan cheese, freshly grated
1 sheet frozen puff pastry dough (half of a 17.3-oz package), thawed

Prep time: 75 minutes
Per serving: 820 calories
30 g protein / 49 g fat / 65 g carbohydrates

1 Put the tuna in a bowl and crush with a fork. Add in the garbanzo beans and mix well.

2 Peel and mince the garlic and add it to the bowl. Season generously with thyme, oregano, salt, and pepper. In another bowl, blend the sour cream with the eggs, then stir in half of the Parmesan cheese.

3 Preheat the oven to 400°F. Lightly dust a work surface with flour. With a rolling pin, roll out the dough, starting from the center and moving to the edges, trying to nudge the dough into an approximate 11-inch circle. Add a sprinkling of flour if necessary to prevent sticking. Carefully transfer the dough to a 10-inch pan. With your fingers, smooth any wrinkles. Trim the dough edges even with the pan.

4 Distribute the garbanzo bean-tuna mixture in the crust, pour the egg mixture on top and sprinkle evenly with the remaining Parmesan. Bake until the filling is set and the crust is golden brown, about 40 minutes.

Serving suggestions: This goes well with Tomato Sauce with Capers or Feta Sauce with Olives, page 29.

Sausage & Sauerkraut Tart

● easy
○ inexpensive

Serves 4
1 onion
1 tbs canola oil
7 oz smoked sausage
1 jar sauerkraut (16 oz), drained
1/2 cup white wine (or chicken stock)
1 bay leaf
Salt & pepper to taste
1 pkg chilled ready-made pizza dough (10 oz)
10 oz sour cream
1 egg

Prep time: 60 minutes
Per serving: 530 calories
15 g protein / 33 g fat / 38 g carbohydrates

1 Peel and dice the onion. In a skillet, heat the oil over medium heat and sauté the onion until translucent. Remove the skin from the sausage and dice. Add the sausage to the pan and sauté with the onion for 5 minutes.

2 Press the excess moisture out of the sauerkraut, and add it to the skillet with the white wine. Add the bay leaf, and season with salt and pepper. Cover and simmer for 10 minutes. Drain the sauerkraut mixture through a colander.

3 Preheat the oven to 400°F. Lightly dust a work surface with flour. With a rolling pin, roll out the dough, starting from the center and moving to the edges, trying to nudge the dough into an approximate 11-inch circle. Add a sprinkling of flour if necessary to prevent sticking. Carefully transfer the dough to a 10-inch pan. With your fingers, smooth any wrinkles. Trim the dough edges even with the pan.

4 Remove the bay leaf and press the moisture out of the sauerkraut mixture. In a large bowl, mix the sour cream and egg, stir in the sauerkraut mixture, and distribute in the crust. Bake the tart until the filling is set and the crust is golden brown, about 30 minutes.

above: Sausage & Sauerkraut Tart
below: Tuna & Garbanzo Bean Quiche

Feta & Olive Quiche

● easy
● vegetarian

Serves 4

16 oz cream cheese
8 oz feta cheese
2 tbs olive oil
3 eggs
5 cloves garlic
1 bunch fresh parsley
1 bunch fresh basil
Salt & pepper to taste
Pinch of cayenne pepper
3 1/2 oz pimiento-stuffed
   olives (about 1/2 of a
   7 oz jar)
One 9- to 10-inch ready-
   made pie crust (in an
   aluminum pan)

Prep time: 60 minutes
Per serving: 870 calories
36 g protein / 59 g fat / 55 g
carbohydrates

1 With a mixer, blend the cream cheese with the feta and olive oil. Blend in the eggs.

2 Peel and mince the garlic and add it to the mixing bowl. Wash the parsley and basil, strip the leaves, finely chop them,. and mix with the cheese mixture. Season generously with salt, pepper, and cayenne.

3 Drain the olives, coarsely slice, and mix with the cheese mixture.

4 Preheat the oven to 400°F. Pour the filling into the crust and smooth the surface. Bake the quiche until the filling is set and lightly browned, about 30-35 minutes.

Serving suggestions:
Accompany with a simple salad of lettuce, tomatoes, cucumber and bell pepper, or Spicy Red Pepper Sauce, page 29.

Variations

Sauté 9 oz grated zucchini in olive oil for 5 minutes and mix with the cheese mixture (you'll only need 8 oz of cream cheese for this version).
Instead of feta, use half Gorgonzola and half mascarpone cheese. Sprinkle 1 bunch of finely chopped basil on top of the baked quiche.

Two-Cheese Quiche

● easy
● sophisticated

Serves 4
5 oz Parmesan cheese, freshly grated
5 oz cheddar cheese, freshly grated
1 tbs flour
1 1/3 cups heavy cream
3 eggs
Salt & pepper to taste
Pinch of freshly grated nutmeg
1 clove garlic
1 bunch fresh chives
1 sheet frozen puff pastry dough (half of a 17.3-oz package), thawed

Prep time: 50 minutes
Per serving: 920 calories
33 g protein / 70 g fat / 39 g carbohydrates

1 In a bowl, mix the Parmesan and cheddar cheese with the flour.

2 In another bowl, blend the cream and eggs, and season with salt, pepper, and nutmeg.

3 Peel and mince the garlic and add to the egg mixture. Wash and finely chop the chives and stir into the egg mixture.

4 Preheat the oven to 425°F. Lightly dust a work surface with flour. With a rolling pin, roll out the dough, starting from the center and moving to the edges, trying to nudge the dough into an approximate 11-inch circle. Add a sprinkling of flour if necessary to prevent sticking. Carefully transfer the dough to a 10-inch pan. With your fingers, smooth any wrinkles. Trim the dough edges even with the pan.

5 Distribute the grated cheese evenly in the crust and pour the egg mixture on top. Bake until the filling is set and the crust is golden brown, about 30 minutes.

Tip! This quiche is hearty and filling. Served with a salad, it makes a complete meal. Or, you can cut it into smaller pieces and include it as part of a multi-course meal. Serve a vegetable soup with fresh herbs as a starter, and poached pears with zabaglione for dessert or a refreshing fruit salad (see the recipe on page 17).

Green Bean Quiche

● good for guests
● easy

Serves 4
6 oz bacon
1 large onion
Salt & pepper to taste
Pinch of dried thyme
2 eggs
7 oz herbed cheese spread,
   such as Boursin
2/3 cup crème fraîche
Salt & pepper to taste
1 tsp hot paprika
20 oz frozen green beans,
   thawed
One 9- to 10-inch ready-
   made pie crust (in an
   aluminum pan)

Prep time: 55 minutes
Per serving: 600 calories
25 g protein / 35 g fat / 45 g
carbohydrates

1 In a skillet, sauté the bacon over medium heat until most of the fat has been melted.

2 Meanwhile, peel and dice the onion. Add the diced onion to the pan with the bacon and sauté until the onion is translucent. Season with salt, pepper, and thyme, and remove the pan from the heat.

3 In a bowl, blend the eggs, herbed cheese, and crème fraîche. Season the mixture with salt, pepper, and paprika.

4 Preheat the oven to 400°F. Distribute the green beans in a star shape in the crust, and sprinkle the bacon-onion mixture evenly on top. Pour the egg-milk mixture on top of all ingredients. Bake the quiche until the filling is set and the crust is golden brown, about 30 minutes.

Corn Quiche with Smoked Sausage

● easy
● inexpensive

Serves 4
8 oz smoked sausage
1 tbs canola oil
2 red bell peppers
3 cans corn (7 oz each),
   drained
2 eggs
2 oz Gouda cheese, freshly
   grated
Salt & pepper to taste
Pinch of hot paprika
1 sheet frozen puff pastry
   (half of 17.3-oz
   package), thawed

Prep time: 65 minutes
Per serving: 770 calories
21 g protein / 52 g fat / 59 g
carbohydrates

1 Slice the smoked sausage, removing the casings if necessary. In a skillet, heat the oil over medium heat and lightly pan-fry the sausage for 2 minutes; set aside and let the mixture cool.

2 Clean, wash, and dice the bell peppers. In a blender or food processor, puree half of the corn until smooth. Add the eggs and Gouda, blend briefly, and season with salt, pepper, and paprika.

3 In a bowl, mix the remaining corn with the diced bell pepper.

4 Preheat the oven to 400°F. Lightly dust a work surface with flour. With a rolling pin, roll out the dough, starting from the center and moving to the edges, trying to nudge the dough into an approximate 11-inch circle. Add a sprinkling of flour if necessary to prevent sticking. Carefully transfer the dough to a 10-inch pan. With your fingers, smooth any wrinkles. Trim the dough edges even with the pan.

5 Distribute the sausage slices evenly in the crust. Scatter the corn-bell pepper mixture over the sausage and pour the egg mixture on top. Bake until the filling is set and the crust is golden brown, about 35 minutes.

above: Green Bean Quiche
below: Corn Quiche with
Smoked Sausage

Brussels Sprout Quiche

● easy
● make ahead

Serves 4
20 oz frozen Brussels
   sprouts
Salt
8 oz sliced bacon
1 bunch fresh chives
3 eggs
1 1/3 cups heavy cream
Salt & pepper to taste
1 tsp hot paprika
Pinch of freshly grated
   nutmeg
4 oz Gouda cheese, freshly
   grated
1 sheet frozen puff pastry
   (half of a 17.3-oz
   package), thawed

Prep time: 65 minutes
Per serving: 885 calories
33 g protein / 64 g fat / 47 g
carbohydrates

1 Cook the Brussels
sprouts in boiling salted
water following the
package directions. Drain,
plunge into ice water,
and drain well.

2 Dice the bacon and fry
it in a skillet until crisp.
Drain on paper towels
and crumble into large
pieces. Wash and finely
chop the chives.

3 In a bowl, blend the
eggs with the cream, and
season generously with
salt, pepper, paprika, and
nutmeg. Stir in the
cheese and chives.

4 Preheat the oven to
425°F. Lightly dust a work
surface with flour. With a
rolling pin, roll out the
dough, starting from the
center and moving to the
edges, trying to nudge
the dough into an
approximate 11-inch
circle. Add a sprinkling of
flour if necessary to
prevent sticking. Carefully
transfer the dough to a
10-inch pan. With your
fingers, smooth any
wrinkles. Trim the dough
edges even with the pan.

5 Distribute the Brussels
sprouts and bacon in the
crust and pour the egg-
cheese filling over the
top. Bake the quiche until
the filling is set and the
crust is golden brown,
about 30 minutes.

Serving suggestion:
Accompany this with
Tomato Sauce with
Capers, page 29.

Two-Mushroom Quiche

● easy
● sophisticated

Serves 4
2 medium leeks (about
   14 oz)
2 tbs butter
18 oz white mushrooms
8 oz oyster mushrooms
2 cloves garlic
Salt & pepper to taste
Pinch of cayenne pepper
1 tsp dried rosemary
1 sheet frozen puff pastry
   (half of a 17.3-oz
   package), thawed
10 oz sour cream
3 eggs
Pinch of freshly grated
   nutmeg

Prep time: 70 minutes
Per serving: 720 calories
16 g protein / 51 g fat / 52 g
carbohydrates

1 Trim the leeks, halve
them lengthwise, wash
well, and cut into narrow
strips. In a wide skillet,
melt the butter over low
heat and sauté the leek
strips for 10 minutes.

2 Meanwhile, trim and
clean all of the
mushrooms. Quarter the
white mushrooms, and
slice the oyster
mushrooms into narrow
strips. Peel and mince the
garlic. Add the
mushrooms and garlic to
the skillet, and sauté over
medium heat until nearly
all of the moisture has
evaporated. Season
generously with salt,
pepper, cayenne, and
rosemary. Remove the pan
from the heat and let the
mixture cool slightly.

3 Preheat oven to 400°F.
Lightly dust a work
surface with flour. With a
rolling pin, roll out the
dough, starting from the
center and moving to the
edges, trying to nudge
the dough into an

approximate 11-inch circle. Add a sprinkling of flour if necessary to prevent sticking. Carefully transfer the dough to a 10-inch pan. With your fingers, smooth any wrinkles. Trim the dough edges even with the pan.

4 Distribute the mushroom mixture evenly in the crust.

5 In a bowl, blend the sour cream and eggs, season generously with salt, pepper, and nutmeg, and pour over the mushroom filling. Bake until the filling is set and the crust is golden brown, about 40 minutes.

above: Two-Mushroom Quiche
below: Brussels Sprout Quiche

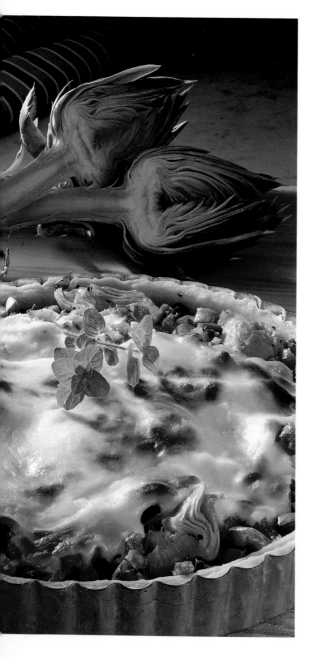

Artichoke Tart

● easy
● sophisticated

Serves 4
16 oz artichoke hearts
(do not choose
marinated)
5 oz unsliced salami
1 green bell pepper
1 sheet frozen puff pastry
(half of a 17.3-oz
package), thawed
Salt & pepper to taste
1 tsp dried oregano
2 oz Parmesan cheese,
freshly grated
1 cup crème fraîche

Prep time: 45 minutes
Per serving: 820 calories
21 g protein / 60 g fat / 51 g
carbohydrates

1 Drain the artichoke
hearts well in a colander.
Peel and dice the salami.
Wash, halve, trim, and
dice the bell pepper.

2 Preheat oven to 400°F.
Lightly dust a work
surface with flour. With a
rolling pin, roll out the
dough, starting from the
center and moving to the
edges, trying to nudge
the dough into an
approximate 11-inch
circle. Add a sprinkling of
flour if necessary to
prevent sticking. Carefully
transfer the dough to a
10-inch pan. With your
fingers, smooth any
wrinkles. Trim the dough
edges even with the pan.

3 Halve the artichoke
hearts lengthwise,
distribute them flat-side
down in the crust, and
season with salt, pepper,
and oregano. Scatter the
chopped salami and bell
pepper between the
artichoke pieces.

4 In a bowl, blend
Parmesan with the crème
fraîche, season with salt
and pepper, and pour
evenly into the crust.
Bake the tart until the
filling is set and the crust
is golden brown, about
25 minutes.

Serving suggestion:
Serve with Gorgonzola
Sauce, or Tomato Sauce
with Capers, page 29.

Herbed Quiche

● easy
● vegetarian

Serves 4
1 bunch fresh Italian
  parsley
1 bunch fresh chives
16 oz cream cheese,
  softened
1/4 cup heavy cream
3 eggs
Salt & pepper to taste
Pinch of hot paprika
2 cloves garlic
One 9- to10-inch ready-
  made pie crust (in an
  aluminum pan)

Prep time: 55 minutes
Per serving: 760 calories
34 g protein / 42 g fat / 68 g
carbohydrates

Variations
For a more substantial
quiche, dice 2 onions and
sauté with 6 oz diced
smoked bacon. Stir into the
cheese mixture.
Instead of parsley and
chives, finely chop 1 bunch
of green onions, sauté in 1
tbs butter for 2 to 3
minutes, and stir them into
the cheese mixture.

1 Preheat the oven to
400°F. Wash and finely
chop the herbs. In a bowl,
blend the cream cheese
with the cream, eggs, and
herbs, and season
generously with salt,
pepper, and paprika. Peel
and mince the garlic and
mix in into the egg
mixture.

2 Distribute the filling in
the crust and spread the
top evenly. Bake until the
filling is set and the crust
is golden brown, about
30 minutes.

Serving suggestion:
Accompany with Tomato
Salad with Green Onions,
page 17.

Traditional Savory Tarts

Savory tarts are popular in many countries: in Switzerland they're called *wähe*, in France they're *tartes* or *galettes*, and in Alsace and Germany they're called *kuche* or *kuchen*. They are usually baked in round pans or dishes or sometimes on a baking sheet—especially when cooking for large numbers of people. Quiches are a version of savory tarts, made with a custard filling of eggs, grated cheese, and milk or cream. These are popular the world over.

Tips and Tricks

• If you plan to use a baking sheet, it's best to roll out the dough directly on a parchment-lined baking sheet.
• You can make any kind of crust in advance and freeze it on the baking sheet. Be sure to wrap it well before putting it into the freezer.
• If your filling is especially moist, like the one used for Quiche Lorraine or other quiches with a yogurt or cream cheese filling, it's wise to prebake or "blind bake" the crust to prevent it

from becoming soggy. This is really important if you plan to serve the quiche cold. **To blind bake a pastry crust:** Line a pan with the desired pastry. Prick the pastry in several places with a fork and line with parchment paper or aluminum foil. Fill with about 12-16 oz of pie weights or dried beans or legumes. Bake at 400°F for 15-20 minutes, until the crust is light golden brown and firm.

• Take care not to overwork pastry dough or it will get tough. Also, make sure the ingredients are cold and try to keep your hands cool and dry while working.
• If you are having a hard time rolling out pastry dough, try just pressing the dough into and up the sides of the pan with your fingers.

About Cheese

Certain types of cheese are especially good for quiches and savory tarts.

Appenzeller

This cow's-milk cheese has an aromatic, fruity taste. It comes from the Appenzell canton in Switzerland.

Emmentaller

Your typical Swiss cheese, complete with holes, from Bern province in Switzerland. Made from cow's milk, it has a mildly aromatic, nutty flavor.

Gorgonzola

From northern Italy, this is a sharp, strongly aromatic blue cheese. Mix it with mascarpone to mellow its assertive flavor.

Gouda

From Holland, Gouda's mild, fruity-nutty flavor blends well with other ingredients.

Mozzarella (fresh)

This usually comes in balls packed in lightly salted whey. Originally made exclusively from the milk of water buffaloes, it's now mostly made from cow's milk. Buffalo Mozzarella is very expensive but the flavor is wonderful for tarts.

Parmesan

Italy's most famous hard cheese, from the Parma province. Parmesan has a distinctive, sharply aromatic, nutty flavor. You can buy Parmesan grated, but it tastes better if you buy it by the chunk and grate it as you go.

Roquefort

A French blue cheese made from sheep's milk, laced with dark blue veins. It has a very distinctive flavor.

Mozzarella, Gorgonzola, Roquefort, Gouda, Parmesan, Appenzeller, Emmentaller, herbed cheese.

Vegetable Tart with Gorgonzola

● takes a while
● vegetarian

Serves 4
Basic Pastry, page 9
26 1/2 oz large tomatoes
1 red bell pepper
1 green bell pepper
1 bunch green onions
1 clove garlic
1 tbs olive oil
Salt & pepper to taste
Pinch of cayenne pepper
5 oz Gorgonzola cheese
1 cup crème fraîche

Prep time: 80 minutes
Per serving: 670 calories
22 g protein / 42 g fat / 54 g
carbohydrates

1 Make the pastry and use it to line a 10-inch pan. Refrigerate until ready to use.

2 Preheat the oven to 400°F. Core the tomatoes. Briefly plunge the tomatoes into boiling water to loosen the skins. Remove skins and cut the tomatoes into eighths. Wash, halve, and trim the bell peppers, then cut them into strips.

3 Trim, wash, and chop the green onions. Peel and mince the garlic. In a skillet, heat the oil over medium heat. Sauté the bell peppers and green onions for 3 minutes. Stir in the garlic and sauté briefly. Season the mixture with salt, pepper, and cayenne. Gently mix in the tomatoes.

4 Distribute the vegetable mixture in the crust.

5 In a bowl, crush the Gorgonzola using a fork. Mix the crème fraîche with the Gorgonzola and distribute on top of the vegetable filling. Bake until golden brown, about 40 minutes.

Serving suggestion:
Cucumber Salad with Dill and Sesame, page 17, is a good companion.

Quiche Lorraine

● good for guests
● make ahead

Serves 4
Rich Pastry 2, page 11
8 oz thick slices smoked bacon
3 eggs
1 1/3 cups crème fraîche
6 oz Gruyère cheese, freshly grated
Salt & pepper to taste
Pinch of freshly grated nutmeg

Prep time: 65 minutes
Per serving: 960 calories
28 g protein / 72 g fat / 49 g
carbohydrates

1 Make the pastry and use it to line a 10-inch pan. Refrigerate until ready to use.

2 Preheat the oven to 400°F. Dice the bacon. Cook the bacon in a pot of boiling water for 2 minutes. Pour through a colander, then drain well on paper towels.

3 In a bowl, blend the eggs and crème fraîche, and stir in the Gruyère cheese. Season with just a tad of salt (bacon is already salty), and pepper and nutmeg.

4 Distribute the bacon in the crust. Pour the egg-crème fraîche mixture evenly on top of the bacon. Bake until the eggs are set and the crust is golden brown, about 35 minutes.

Tip! Lorraine refers to the region of France where this quiche was invented.

top: Vegetable Tart with Gorgonzola
bottom: Quiche Lorraine

Tarte Provençal

- takes a while
- vegetarian

Serves 4
Rich Pastry 2, page 11
1 onion
3 cloves garlic
1/4 cup olive oil
1 small eggplant (about
  9 oz)
2 zucchini (about 9 oz)
1 red bell pepper
1 yellow bell pepper
2 large tomatoes
Salt & pepper to taste
1 tsp dried oregano
1 tsp dried thyme
1 tsp dried rosemary
3 oz Parmesan cheese,
  freshly grated

Prep time: 90 minutes
Per serving: 700 calories
20 g protein / 41 g fat / 66 g
carbohydrates

1 Make the pastry and use it to line a 10-inch pan. Blind bake the pastry (see page 52) and set it aside.

2 Preheat the oven to 400°F. Peel and dice the onion. Peel and mince the garlic. In a large skillet, heat the oil over medium heat and sauté the onion until translucent. Add the garlic and sauté briefly.

3 Meanwhile, wash, trim, and cube the eggplant and zucchini. Add the cubes to the pan and sauté for 10 minutes.

4 Wash, trim, and dice the bell peppers. Core the tomatoes. Briefly plunge the tomatoes into boiling water to loosen the skins. Remove the skins and coarsely chop the tomatoes. Add the bell peppers and tomatoes to the skillet. Season with salt, pepper, and the herbs. Simmer the vegetable mixture uncovered for 15 minutes. Cool well.

5 Season the vegetables to taste and mix in half of the Parmesan. Distribute the mixture in the crust and scatter the rest of the Parmesan on top. Bake until golden brown, about 25 minutes.

Pissaladière

(Niçoise-style
vegetable tart)

- sophisticated
- good for guests

Serves 4
Rich Pastry 2, page 11
2 large onions
3 cloves garlic
5 tbs olive oil
Salt & pepper to taste
2 tsp thyme, fresh or dried
20 oz tomatoes
3 1/2 oz small black olives,
  pitted
2 cans anchovy fillets (2 oz
  cans)

Prep time: 80 minutes
Per serving: 690 calories
18 g protein / 42 g fat / 62 g
carbohydrates

1 Make the pastry and use it to line a 10-inch pan. Refrigerate until ready to use.

2 Preheat the oven to 400°F. Peel and dice the onions. Peel and mince the garlic. In a skillet, heat 3 tbs of the oil over medium heat and sauté the onions until translucent. Season with salt, pepper, and half of the thyme. Add the garlic, reduce the heat to very low, and sauté all ingredients until soft, about 15 minutes.

3 Core the tomatoes. Briefly plunge the tomatoes into boiling water to loosen the skins. Remove the skins and slice the tomatoes.

4 Distribute the onion mixture evenly in the crust. Cover with the tomato slices, and drizzle with the remaining 2 tbs olive oil. Season with salt, pepper, and the remaining thyme. Scatter the olives over the top. Bake until light golden brown, about 30 minutes. Distribute the anchovy fillets on top and bake for 5 more minutes.

above: Tarte Provençal
below: Pissaladière

Camembert Tart

● good for guests
● vegetarian

Serves 4
Rich Pastry 2, page 11
1 large onion
1 tbs softened butter
16 oz ripe Camembert
cheese
2 oz butter, softened
Salt & pepper to taste
1 tsp hot paprika
1 egg

Prep time: 60 minutes
Per serving: 940 calories
32 g protein / 68 g fat / 50 g
carbohydrates

1 Make the pastry and use it to line a 10-inch pan. Refrigerate until ready to use.

2 Preheat the oven to 400°F. Peel and dice the onion. In a skillet, melt the butter over medium heat and sauté the onion until soft. Transfer to a bowl. Cut off the Camembert rind. Cut the cheese into pieces and crush well using a fork. Add to the bowl and mix well with the butter and sautéed onion. Season with salt, pepper, and paprika and cool slightly. Stir in the egg.

3 Spread the cheese filling evenly in the crust and bake the tart until golden brown, about 25 to 30 minutes.

Tip! Camembert is a soft ripened cow's milk cheese. Choose one that is fat and slightly soft. You can also use Brie for this recipe

German-Style Onion Tart

● takes a while
● inexpensive

Serves 6
10 oz thick-sliced smoked
  bacon
1 tbs butter
4 1/2 lb onions
Salt & pepper to taste
2 tsp caraway seeds
2 pkg refrigerated bread
  or pizza dough (10-oz
  pkg), or use your favorite
  homemade recipe
20 oz sour cream
5 eggs

Prep time: 135 minutes
Per serving: 860 calories
32 g protein / 50 g fat / 71 g
carbohydrates

1 Dice the bacon. In a
large skillet, melt the
butter over medium-low
heat. Add the bacon and
sauté until most of the
fat is melted. Peel and
dice the onions, and add
them to the skillet.
Season with salt, pepper,
and caraway seeds and
sauté for 15 minutes,
until soft. Remove from
the heat and cool.

2 Preheat the oven to
400°F. Grease a baking
sheet and roll out the
dough directly on the
sheet. Fold up the ends of
the dough to make a
raised dough edge.

3 In a bowl, blend the
sour cream and eggs, mix
in the onion mixture, and
distribute the filling
evenly on top of the
crust. Bake until golden
brown, about 45 minutes.

Tip! For wonderful
flavor, choose bacon that
has been smoked over
aromatic wood, such as
applewood. Look for it in
a specialty foods store.

Middle Eastern-Style Lamb Tart

● sophisticated
● takes a while

Serves 4
Basic Pastry, page 9
2 tbs canola oil
20 oz ground lamb
1 medium-sized eggplant
1 large onion
3 cloves garlic
2 large tomatoes
2 oz raisins
2 tbs chopped almonds
Salt & pepper to taste
Pinch of cumin
1/2 tsp ground cinnamon
1 tsp grated lemon zest
4 oz feta cheese

Prep time: 80 minutes
Per serving: 940 calories
32 g protein / 64 g fat / 62 g
carbohydrates

1 Make the pastry and use it to line a 10-inch pan. Refrigerate until ready to use.

2 Preheat the oven to 400°F. In a large skillet, heat the oil over medium heat and lightly sauté the ground lamb until crumbly and brown, about 10 minutes.

3 Wash the eggplant, remove the stem, and chop into 1/2-inch cubes. Peel and dice the onion and garlic. Add the eggplant, onion, and garlic to the skillet and simmer.

4 Core the tomatoes. Briefly plunge the tomatoes into boiling water to loosen the skins. Remove skins and seeds, and coarsely chop the tomatoes. Add the tomatoes to the skillet with the raisins and almonds. Season generously with salt, pepper, cumin, cinnamon, and lemon zest, cover and simmer for 20 minutes. Crumble the feta and mix into the ingredients in the skillet. Cool slightly.

5 Distribute the lamb-vegetable filling evenly in the crust. Bake the tart until golden brown, about 30 minutes.

Serving suggestion: Serve with Herbed Yogurt Sauce, page 29.

Swiss-Style Cheese and Grape Quiche

● vegetarian
● good for guests

Serves 4
Cream Cheese Pastry, page 6
18 oz seedless green grapes
1 cup heavy cream
3 eggs
4 oz Gruyère cheese, freshly grated
Salt & pepper to taste
Pinch of ground caraway seeds

Prep time: 75 minutes
Per serving: 845 calories
24 g protein / 53 g fat / 73 g
carbohydrates

1 Make the pastry and use it to line a 10-inch pan. Refrigerate until ready to use.

2 Preheat the oven to 400°F. Wash the grapes, drain well, and peel them if desired.

3 In a bowl, blend the cream, eggs, and half of the cheese. Season with salt, pepper, and the caraway seeds.

4 Distribute the grapes in the crust and sprinkle the remaining cheese on top. Pour the cream-egg mixture over the grapes.

Bake until the filling is set and the crust is golden brown, about 40 minutes.

Tip! If you can't find Gruyère cheese at the market, choose another type of high-quality Swiss cheese, such as Appenzeller, Emmentaller. or a good domestic Swiss-style cheese.

above: Middle Eastern-Style Lamb Tart
below: Swiss-Style Cheese and Grape Quiche

Credits

Published originally under the title Quiches, ©1997 Gräfe und Unzer Verlag GmbH, Munich
English translation for the U.S. market ©2000, Silverback Books, Inc.

Editors: Jennifer Newens, CCP, Vené Franco
Translator: Jacolyn Harmer
Design and production: Shanti Nelson
Design: Heinz Kraxenberger
Photos: Odette Teubner

Printed in Hong Kong through Global Interprint, Santa Rosa, California
ISBN 1-930603-60-6

Cornelia Adam
Adam originally worked in the hotel and catering business, during which time she traveled to many foreign countries. Later she was able to utilize these various job-related experiences as editor of a well-known German women's magazine. Currently she works as a freelance food journalist and cookbook author.

Odette Teubner
Teubner grew up among cameras, flood lights, and experimental kitchens. She received her education from her father, the internationally known food photographer Christian Teubner. After a brief excursion into the field of fashion, she returned to the field of food, and has since had the rare fortune to combine profession and hobby.